PRICE ACTION DAY TRADING

Mastering Day Trading Through Price Action Strategies

— CHINEDU BROWN

PRICE ACTION DAY TRADING

2024 CHINEDU BROWN

All rights reserved. No part of this work may be reproduced or transmitted in any form or by any means without written permission from the publisher unless otherwise indicated.

To say thank you for purchasing this book, I offer you a free

Video Course and more as a token of appreciation

Find the link to the Video Course at the end of this book.

Table of Contents

INTRODUCTION _____ vi

Introduction to Price Action Trading _____ vi

The Evolution of Day Trading _____ vii

Understanding Price Action Fundamentals _____ vii

Why Does Price Action Matter in Forex Markets _____ viii

Personal Trading Philosophy & Mindset _____ ix

The Path Forward _____ ix

ONE _____ 1

Fundamental Technical Analysis Principles _____ 1

Candlestick Patterns and their Significance _____ 2

Support and Resistance Dynamics _____ 2

Market Structure and Trend Identification _____ 3

Understanding Price Movement Like a Professional Trader __ 4

TWO _____ 6

Core Price Action Trading Strategies _____ 6

Pin Bar Strategy Explained _____ 6

Inside-Bar Trading Techniques _____ 7

Engulfing Candle Setups _____ 8

Breakout and Rejection Trade Configurations _____ 9

Combining Strategies to Increase Effectiveness _____ 10

Practice Core Strategies _____10

THREE _____12

Risk Management and Trading Psychology _____12

Calculating Precise Position Sizes_____12

Establishing Strategic Stop-Loss Levels _____14

Managing Emotional Impulses_____15

Developing a Disciplined Trading Approach_____15

Risk-reward ratios and probabilities_____16

Psychological Aspects of Winning and Losing_____17

FOUR _____19

Advanced Chart Pattern Recognition_____19

Identifying High Probability Chart Formations_____20

Triangle and Wedge Pattern Trading_____20

Head and Shoulder Pattern Analysis _____22

Complex Harmonic Trading Patterns _____23

Tips for Identifying and Trading Patterns _____23

FIVE _____25

Timing and Entry Precision _____25

Confirmation Signal Techniques _____26

Multi-Timeframe Analysis _____27

Detecting High-Confluence Entry Points_____28

Trade Execution Strategies _____29

Balancing Precision and Flexibility_____30

SIX_____32

Technical Indicators and Price Action _____32

Complementary Indicator Selection_____33

Moving Averages in Price Action Context. _____34

Momentum oscillators _____35

Volume Analysis Techniques _____36

Integrating Indicators and Price Action _____37

SEVEN _____39

Trading Plan Development _____39

Creating a Personal Trading Blueprint_____39

Performance Tracking and Journaling _____41

Backtesting and Strategy refinement _____42

Developing Consistent Trading Habits _____43

EIGHT _____45

Market Context and Economic Considerations _____45

Understanding Forex Market Dynamics. _____46

The Effect of Economic News on Price Action_____47

Session-Based Trading Strategies._____48

Adapting to changing market conditions. _____49

CONCLUSION _____51

The Path to Trading Mastery _____51

Synthesizing Learnt Strategies _____51

Continuous Learning and Adaptation._____52

Establishing Long-Term Trading Consistency_____53

The Future of Price Action Trading _____55

Final Words _____56

INTRODUCTION

INTRODUCTION TO PRICE ACTION TRADING

At 3 a.m., the faint glow from my laptop screen filled the tiny apartment living room. My hands trembled slightly as I watched another trading position turn into red numbers. Another $500 is gone—just like that. This wasn't just money; these were dreams fading in front of my eyes.

My foray into forex trading began not with success, but with a string of terrible, humiliating failures that would shape my understanding of financial markets. Back then, I was like most new traders: full of enthusiasm, drowning in complexity, and fundamentally misunderstanding how markets really work.

THE EVOLUTION OF DAY TRADING

Day trading is more than just a job; it's an art form that requires precision, psychological resilience, and a thorough understanding of market dynamics. Traditional trading methods can overwhelm newbies with sophisticated indicators, algorithmic algorithms, and confusing technical analysis. Price action trading cuts through the noise, providing a clear view of market movement.

Price action trading is a paradigm shift away from traditional indicator-based methods. Instead than relying on lagging technical indicators that simply reinterpret prior market moves, price action traders read the market's language directly using candlestick patterns, support and resistance levels, and raw price behavior.

UNDERSTANDING PRICE ACTION FUNDAMENTALS

Understanding market psychology is the bedrock of price action trading. Each candlestick represents a struggle between buyers and sellers, institutional momentum, and retail trader mood. These price swings are not arbitrary; they are a reflection of collective market psychology, compacted into visual representations on a graph.

Consider a conventional pin bar formation: a candle with a long tail pointing in one direction, indicating a potential reversal. This is more than just a pattern; it's a story of market participants changing their minds about the worth of an item. Professional traders see more than just lines and colors; they notice tales about supply, demand, and market sentiment.

WHY DOES PRICE ACTION MATTER IN FOREX MARKETS

Forex markets are unique ecosystems for global economic relationships. Unlike stock markets, which are limited to certain exchanges, forex trades 24 hours a day, across many worldwide sessions. Price action becomes your common language in this complex environment.

My early trading losses taught me that complicated does not equal effective. I spent thousands on advanced trading software, paid for pricey signal providers, and pursued every "guaranteed" trading approach. What was the result? Consistent losses and increasing frustration.

The insight came when I took everything down to its most fundamental level: monitoring pure price movement. No more crowded charts with numerous conflicting indications. Simply clean, straightforward price action that conveyed market intentions with extraordinary precision.

PERSONAL TRADING PHILOSOPHY & MINDSET

Successful trading requires more than just technical skills; it is primarily a mental discipline. The markets are unconcerned about your wants; they respond to group behavior. Your role as a trader is to become an objective observer, removing emotional attachments from financial judgements.

This Needs Developing:

- Emotional Detachment From Particular Trades.
- Consistent Risk Management.
- Adaptability To Changing Market Conditions.
- Continuous Education And Self-Improvement

PRICE ACTION DAY TRADING

THE PATH FORWARD

"Price Action Day Trading" is more than just a book of tactics; it's a road map for changing your connection with financial markets. We'll breakdown price action trading, reducing complicated principles to actionable, understandable frameworks.

Remember, every great trader started out as a beginner trying to make sense of the market pandemonium. Your path begins with understanding that trading is a talent, not a lottery. With dedication, focus, and the correct expertise, you can create a solid trading strategy that provides consistent, long-term profits.

The complex realm of price action trading, teaching you the tools, strategies, and psychological frameworks required to traverse forex markets with confidence and precision.

The markets are waiting. Are you prepared to speak their language?

XIII

CHINEDU BROWN

ONE

FUNDAMENTAL TECHNICAL ANALYSIS PRINCIPLES

To trade efficiently with price action, you must first understand the fundamental concepts of technical analysis. These concepts are the foundation of any effective trading strategy, particularly in the forex market. While other traders rely primarily on indicators or automated methods, price action traders concentrate on the actual movement of prices.

This chapter will walk you through key technical principles and help you develop the abilities necessary to interpret the market's story.

CANDLESTICK PATTERNS AND THEIR SIGNIFICANCE

Candlestick patterns are one of the first things a price action trader needs to grasp. Candlesticks are more than just colorful representations of price movement; they also provide important information about market emotion. Each candlestick tells a story—a conflict between buyers and sellers. For example, a long bullish candle suggests that buyers prevailed during that time period, whereas a long bearish candle implies that sellers were in charge.

Common patterns such as the doji, hammer, and shooting star indicate potential reversals or continuations. I remember staring at charts for hours early on in my trading career, trying to figure out what these patterns represented. One day, I noticed a hammer pattern at a critical support level. With some caution, I entered a long trade, and to my surprise, the price exploded in my favor. That moment solidified my trust in the strength of candlestick patterns.

SUPPORT AND RESISTANCE DYNAMICS

Support and resistance levels serve as the foundation for technical analysis. Support functions as a floor, where prices tend to stop falling, and resistance acts as a ceiling, where prices frequently stop rising. These levels are more than just arbitrary lines; they represent important psychological zones where traders make decisions.

Consider a price chart as a battleground. When the price approaches a significant resistance level, sellers frequently intervene, sending the price back down. In contrast, at a strong support level, buyers emerge, driving the price higher. Recognizing these zones can help you estimate where the price will stall or reverse.

I remember a trade in which I misread a resistance level. I placed a buy order, expecting the price to break through. Instead, it abruptly reversed, incurring a loss. That experience taught me to respect these levels and to await confirmation before entering a trade.

MARKET STRUCTURE AND TREND IDENTIFICATION

Understanding market structure is critical for recognizing trends and trading possibilities. The market cycles through uptrends, downtrends, and consolidation phases. In an uptrend, the price rises to new highs and lows, indicating that buyers have control. In a downtrend, lower highs and lower lows imply seller dominance. Consolidation, on the other hand, occurs when the market swings sideways, giving neither buyers nor sellers an advantage.

To trade efficiently, line your trades with the current trend. I've discovered the hard way that resisting the trend is like swimming upstream—exhausting and frequently unsuccessful. During one trade, I shorted a currency pair in an uptrend, believing it was overextended. The market quickly proven me wrong, and I exited at a big loss. Since then, I've made it a point to trade with the trend.

UNDERSTANDING PRICE MOVEMENT LIKE A PROFESSIONAL TRADER

Reading price movements is a skill that distinguishes inexperienced traders from professionals. Professionals interpret the overall context, not just individual candles or patterns. For example, a bullish engulfing candle near a crucial support level is more significant than the same pattern in the middle of a range.

To improve this talent, concentrate on observing how the price reacts at key levels. Does it bounce sharply or hesitate? Do lengthy wicks signify rejection? The more you practice, the better you'll get at reading price movements intuitively.

I once saw a market in which the price fluctuated around a strong support level. Many inexperienced traders were getting whipsawed and entering transactions too soon. By patiently waiting and studying how the price interacted with the level, I was able to pinpoint the exact time when buyers took control. That trade proved to be one of my most rewarding experiences.

Mastering candlestick patterns, support and resistance, market structure, and price movement will provide a firm basis for your trading career. These principles are interrelated. Candlestick patterns, for example, take on greater significance when they appear at support or resistance levels. Similarly, understanding market structure allows you to evaluate whether a pattern represents a reversal or a continuance.

As you use these strategies to your trading, keep in mind that practice and patience are essential. Spend time analyzing charts, sketching levels, and assessing your understanding. The forex market is dynamic, and no single strategy works every time. However, by adhering to these fundamental rules, you will be better prepared to navigate the market with confidence.

In the next chapter, we'll look at specific price action trading tactics. These strategies build on the fundamentals taught here, providing you with actionable ways to trade the market efficiently.

TWO

CORE PRICE ACTION TRADING STRATEGIES

Price action trading involves reading market fluctuations and using them to make sound trading decisions. In this chapter, we will look at the fundamental price action strategies that you can use to discover chances in the forex market. Each strategy is based on simplicity and practicality, making it suitable for traders who prefer to focus on price action rather than indicators.

PIN BAR STRATEGY EXPLAINED

The pin bar strategy is a popular and effective method for price action trading. A pin bar is a single candlestick pattern with a short body and a long wick that indicates rejection at a specific price level. It indicates a possible reversal or continuance of the trend.

Trading pin bars successfully requires an understanding of their position. A pin bar near a significant support or resistance level has more weight than one formed in the middle of a range. For example, if a bullish pin bar appears near a strong support level, it could suggest that buyers are entering the market, and the price would likely rise.

I have clear memories of my first successful pin bar trade. The EUR/USD pair saw a bullish pin bar form near a well-established support zone. I initiated a long trade with a tight stop-loss below the wick. The price rose sharply, exceeding my profit target within hours. That trade taught me the value of waiting for high-probability setups.

INSIDE-BAR TRADING TECHNIQUES

An inside bar is another effective price action setup. It happens when a smaller candlestick totally fits within the range of the previous candle. This pattern denotes consolidation and can result in a breakout in any direction.

Consider the market context in order to trade inside bars effectively. In a trending market, an inside bar frequently serves as a pause before the trend resumes. In contrast, in a range-bound market, an inside bar near the top or bottom of the range may indicate a reversal.

During one of my early trading days, I noticed an inside bar on the GBP/USD pair in an uptrend. I entered a buy trade after the breakout direction was confirmed by a powerful bullish candle. The price rose, and I withdrew with a substantial profit. This experience highlighted the need of synchronizing inside bar trades with the current trend.

ENGULFING CANDLE SETUPS

Engulfing candles are a traditional reverse pattern. A bullish engulfing candle happens when a larger green candle completely engulfs the previous red candle, indicating high buyer interest. In contrast, a bearish engulfing candle shows seller dominance.

The most effective engulfing setups occur at important support or resistance levels. For example, a bullish engulfing candle near a support level indicates that buyers have taken control and the price is likely to climb. To trade this setup, enter after the engulfing candle has closed, with a stop-loss below the low for bullish setups and above the high for bearish ones.

One memorable trade I executed with this strategy was on the USD/JPY pair. The market had been testing a major resistance level for several days. Finally, a bearish engulfing candle formed, confirming the sellers' supremacy. I entered a short trade and profited significantly as the price dropped progressively.

BREAKOUT AND REJECTION TRADE CONFIGURATIONS

Breakouts and rejections are key ideas in price action trading. A breakout occurs when the price goes decisively past a support or resistance level, whereas a rejection occurs when the price tests a level but does not break through.

To trade breakouts, wait for confirmation. A powerful candle closing above the level suggests a valid breakout. In contrast, for rejection trades, look for indicators of hesitation at the key level, such as long wicks or small-bodied candles.

I once traded a breakout in the AUD/USD pair during an economic data release. The price had been consolidating near a resistance level, and the data served as a catalyst for the breakout. I entered the trade when the price broke through the resistance level, profiting handsomely.

COMBINING STRATEGIES TO INCREASE EFFECTIVENESS

While each of these strategies is effective on their own, they can be combined to produce even better outcomes. For example, a bullish pin bar that forms as part of an inner bar setup at a strong support level indicates a high-confluence trade. Similarly, employing an engulfing candle to confirm a breakout or rejection trade can provide an additional level of certainty.

When using these strategies, keep in mind that no setup is perfect. Always limit your risk with proper position sizing and stop-loss levels. The goal is not to win every trade, but to develop an edge that yields consistent outcomes over time.

PRACTICE CORE STRATEGIES

The only way to perfect these strategies is to practice. Spend some time analyzing historical charts to spot pin bars, inside bars, engulfing candles, and breakouts. Consider how these setups work in various market conditions and how you might have traded them. Before using these strategies in actual trading, practice them on a demo account.

When I first started, I spent hours each day studying charts. I would print screenshots of settings and make notes about what worked and what didn't. This hands-on approach accelerated my learning and given me the confidence to trade for real money.

The strategies presented in this chapter are critical components of your trading arsenal. Mastering the pin bar, inner bar, engulfing candle, and breakout/rejection settings will provide you with a solid basis for navigating the forex market with confidence.

THREE

RISK MANAGEMENT AND TRADING PSYCHOLOGY

Trading is more than just developing profitable strategies; it is also about protecting your capital and having the proper mindset. No matter how amazing your technical analysis or strategies are, trading success will stay elusive until you practice proper risk management and psychological discipline. In this chapter, we will examine the principles of risk management and the mental toughness required to succeed in the Forex market.

CALCULATING PRECISE POSITION SIZES

One of the most important parts of risk management is choosing the appropriate position size for each trade. This ensures that no single loss causes major damage to your account. Position size is the process of determining how much capital to risk on a trade, which is normally a modest percentage of your account balance (1% to 2% every trade).

To compute position size, you need three crucial variables:

- **Account Balance:** represents your overall trading capital.
- **Risk Percentage:** The percentage of your account that you are willing to risk.
- **Stop-Loss Distance:** is the amount of pips between your entry point and stop-loss.

For example, if your account balance is $10,000 and you risk 2%, the risk each trade is $200. If your stop-loss distance is 50 pips, your position size will be computed as $200 divided by 50, which is $4 every pip. Understanding this equation allows you to trade with confidence, without the fear of losing more than you can afford.

I learnt this the hard way early on in my trading career. I ignored the risk and took huge holdings in order to generate quick profits. After a series of losses, my account had dropped by approximately 50%. It was a humbling experience, but it taught me to appreciate the market and put risk management ahead of possible rewards.

ESTABLISHING STRATEGIC STOP-LOSS LEVELS

A stop-loss is an essential tool for any trader. It protects your account from catastrophic losses by automatically terminating trades when the price swings against you. The key to efficient stop-loss placement is a balance of protection and flexibility.

Avoid putting your stop-loss too close to your entry point, as regular market movements may activate it early. In contrast, a stop-loss positioned too far away increases your risk unnecessarily. Ideally, base your stop-loss on technical indicators such as support and resistance levels or recent swing highs and lows.

I once rejected a stop-loss on a trade, sure that the market will eventually turn in my favor. Instead, the price continued to drop, and I watched helplessly as my losses grew. That trade taught me never to trade without a stop loss, no matter how sure I am in the setup.

MANAGING EMOTIONAL IMPULSES

Emotions are the trader's worst adversary. Fear, greed, and frustration can impair judgement, leading to rash judgements. Fear may cause you to abandon a trade prematurely, but greed may encourage you to stay in it for too long. Frustration following a loss may lead you to overtrade in an effort to recover quickly

To manage these impulses, create and stick to a trading strategy. Your plan should include entrance and exit criteria, position sizes, and risk levels. Using a structured approach reduces the chance of emotional trading.

One of my most crucial discoveries occurred following a particularly intense trading session. I had suffered successive losses and wanted to conduct a revenge trade to compensate. Predictably, the trade failed. Reflecting on that experience, I realized the value of taking a break following losses and returning to the market with a fresh perspective.

DEVELOPING A DISCIPLINED TRADING APPROACH

Discipline is the key to long-term trading success. It entails sticking to your trading strategy, even when it is tempting to depart. Accepting losses as a natural part of trading and not allowing them to undermine your confidence is another aspect of discipline.

Keeping a trading journal is a useful practice. Keep a record of every trade you make, including the setup, entry and exit positions, and reasons behind it. Review your journal on a regular basis to find behavioral patterns and opportunities for improvement.

My log revealed that I was constantly starting trades prematurely, leading to unnecessary losses, during one particularly difficult month. Armed with this knowledge, I changed my strategy, waiting for clearer confirmations before taking transactions. This tiny change has a big influence on my overall performance.

RISK-REWARD RATIOS AND PROBABILITIES

Understanding the concept of risk-reward ratios is critical for successful risk management. The risk-reward ratio analyses a trade's prospective profit and loss. A 1:2 ratio, for example, indicates you're risking $1 for a chance to win $2.

Always look for trades with a favorable risk-reward ratio. Even if your success percentage is less than 50%, a constant 1:2 ratio can increase your trading profits over time. For example, if you win 40% of your trades but your winners are twice as large as your losers, you'll still be profitable.

I've had transactions when the setup appeared to be ideal, but the potential profit was insufficient to offset the risk. Early on, I would take such transactions regardless, often with little gains or losses. Now, I've learnt to be patient and wait for situations with high risk-reward potential.

PSYCHOLOGICAL ASPECTS OF WINNING AND LOSING

Trading entails both winning and losing. The goal is to avoid allowing either to have a significant impact on you. A winning streak might lead to overconfidence, prompting you to take needless risks. A losing streak, on the other hand, can undermine your confidence and make you cautious to take advantage of legitimate situations.

After my first huge win, I felt unstoppable and began expanding my position sizes indiscriminately. The market quickly humbled me with a series of losses. That experience taught me to remain grounded and approach each trade separately, regardless of my recent results.

Risk management and trading psychology are interdependent. They work together to build a long-term trading career. You can trade with confidence and resilience if you calculate correct position sizes, establish strategic stop-loss levels, and control your emotions.

In the following chapter, we will look at advanced chart pattern detection, giving you the tools you need to identify high-probability setups and improve your trading.

FOUR

ADVANCED CHART PATTERN RECOGNITION

Mastering chart patterns is an essential ability for every trader looking to thrive at price action trading. Chart patterns are visual representations of market psychology that provide useful insights into potential price movements. In this chapter, we will look at some of the most effective and high-probability chart patterns, including how to identify them, their meaning, and how to trade them efficiently.

By the end of this chapter, you should have a better understanding of chart patterns and the confidence to use them in real-world trading settings.

IDENTIFYING HIGH PROBABILITY CHART FORMATIONS

Chart patterns occur when price action consolidates, reverses, or continues on a trend. High-probability patterns usually appear in places of high market interest, such as near support and resistance levels or following long moves. The key to properly trading these patterns is to spot them early and wait for confirmation before making a trade.

One of my most memorable trades involved recognizing a standard chart pattern: the double bottom. The GBP/USD pair's price had been heading lower but found firm support at a major level, generating two roughly identical troughs. After the neckline was broken, I initiated a long trade, and the price skyrocketed, resulting in one of my finest trades of the month. This experience underlined the importance of recognizing and acting on high-probability setup opportunities.

TRIANGLE AND WEDGE PATTERN TRADING

Triangles and wedges are common continuation and reversal patterns. A triangle pattern occurs when the price consolidates inside converging trendlines, whereas a wedge pattern appears when the range narrows with a sloping direction. These patterns indicate that the market is preparing for a breakout.

- **Ascending Triangle:** This bullish pattern arises when the price makes higher lows and meets a horizontal resistance line. An upward movement could result from a breakout over the resistance line.

- **Descending Triangle:** This bearish pattern features lower highs and a horizontal support line, with a breakout below the support indicating a downward move.

- **Symmetrical Triangle:** This neutral pattern is formed when two trendlines converge symmetrically. The breakout direction is often determined by the current trend.

Trading these patterns demands patience. Wait for a clean breakout and a retest of the breakout level before entering a

PRICE ACTION DAY TRADING

trade. I recall a trade on the EUR/USD pair in which I identified a symmetrical triangle following a heavy downturn. As soon as the price broke below the lower trendline, I entered a short trade, which resulted in a substantial profit when the price fell further.

HEAD AND SHOULDER PATTERN ANALYSIS

The head and shoulders pattern is one of the most consistent reversal patterns. It consists of three peaks: a taller center peak (the head) and two lower peaks (the shoulders). The neckline joins the lower parts of the two shoulders and serves as the breakout level.

- **Standard Head and Shoulders:** Indicates a bearish reversal. The breakout happens when the price falls below the neckline.
- **Inverse Head and Shoulders:** Signifies a bullish reversal. The breakout occurs when the price rises above the neckline.

When trading this pattern, make sure that the breakout is accompanied by significant volume to prove its validity. Following an extended slump, an inverted head and shoulders pattern appeared in one of my USD/JPY trades. When the price broke above the neckline, I took a long position and rode the wave to a major resistance level. That trade gave me even more confidence in the pattern's efficiency.

COMPLEX HARMONIC TRADING PATTERNS

Harmonic patterns are advanced forms that use Fibonacci retracement and extension levels to forecast future price reversals. Gartley, Butterfly, Bat, and Crab are some of the most popular harmonic patterns. While these patterns take more precision and practice to learn, they can yield extremely exact entry and exit spots.

For example, the Gartley pattern uses a special Fibonacci structure in which price retraces to 61.8% before reversing.

Identifying these patterns demands a keen eye and the skill to draw precise Fibonacci levels.

I recall a trade in which I detected a Butterfly pattern on the AUD/USD pair. I found the possible reversal zone and placed a pending order using Fibonacci levels. The trade went exactly as planned, and I met my target within hours. Harmonic patterns require more effort, but the benefits might be well worth it.

TIPS FOR IDENTIFYING AND TRADING PATTERNS

- **Concentrate on Context:** Chart patterns are more dependable when they are consistent with market context. For example, a continuation pattern in a strong trend has a larger chance of success than one in a volatile market.

- **Wait for Confirmation:** Always wait for a breakout or retest to ensure the pattern's validity. Premature entries can result in excessive losses.

- **Combine With Other Tools:** Chart patterns can be verified using support and resistance levels, trend lines, and candlestick patterns.

- **Practice, Practice, Practice:** The more you analyse charts, the more adept you will get at identifying and trading patterns.

Chart patterns provide an insight into market psychology and a framework for making sound trading decisions. Mastering high-probability setups such as triangles, head and shoulders, and harmonic patterns will greatly improve your trading performance.

FIVE

TIMING AND ENTRY PRECISION

In trading, timing is everything. Even the best strategies can fail if you don't time your entry correctly. Chapter 6 focusses on how to improve your entry, boosting your chances of success while reducing risk. Take your price action trading to the next level by mastering timing and entry precision.

This chapter discusses confirmation signal methodologies, various timeframe analysis, detecting high-confluence entry positions, and trade execution strategies. Along the way, I'll share a personal tale to demonstrate the value of precise timing.

CONFIRMATION SIGNAL TECHNIQUES

A confirmation signal is a price action indicator that confirms your trade idea. The market is telling you, "Yes, this is a good entry point." Candlestick patterns, breakouts, and retests of important levels are all common confirmation indications.

For example, a bullish engulfing candle at a strong support level could indicate a reversal and confirm a buy setup. Similarly, a breakout followed by a successful retest of resistance converted to support might verify a trend continuation trade.

Early in my trading career, I frequently entered trades without waiting for confirmation indications. One memorable mistake was entering a short trade on the EUR/USD after noticing a bearish engulfing candle.

However, I neglected the level of support just below. The price bounced off that level and rallied, resulting in a loss on my trade. This event taught me the value of waiting for strong confirmation before pressing the trigger.

MULTI-TIMEFRAME ANALYSIS

Multiple timeframe analysis entails examining the same market over multiple timeframes to acquire a more comprehensive perspective. This strategy allows you to align your trades with the dominating trend while fine-tuning your entries.

- **Higher Timeframe (HTF):** The HTF shows the large picture, including the overall trend and critical levels. For example, the daily chart may show an uptrend with a major resistance zone.

- **Lower Timeframe (LTF):** The LTF allows you to pinpoint specific entry points and confirmation signals. For example, the 1-hour chart may show a bullish breakout and retest of the daily uptrend.

Using several timeframes guarantees that your trades are properly linked with market context. One of my most successful trades involves analyzing the GBP/JPY pair across three timeframes.

The weekly chart indicated an uptrend, the daily chart revealed a consolidation breakout, and the 4-hour chart presented an ideal pullback entry. The synchronization of timeframes provided me the confidence to enter the trade, which proved to be extremely rewarding.

DETECTING HIGH-CONFLUENCE ENTRY POINTS

Confluence refers to the convergence of many factors that support a trade idea. High-confluence setups are effective because they incorporate different aspects of technical analysis, boosting the likelihood of success. *The key confluence factors are:*

- Support and resistance levels, as well as trendlines and channels.
- Fibonacci retracement levels - Price action indicators (e.g. candlestick patterns)

The more factors that align at the same point, the stronger the confluence. However, you should avoid "paralysis by analysis"—not all indicators must concur. Concentrate on a few dependable instruments that function well together.

I recall a trade on the AUD/USD pair that demonstrated the potential of confluence. The price was reaching a critical support level, which coincided with a 61.8% Fibonacci retracement and an ascending trend line. A bullish engulfing candle occurred at this level, providing final confirmation to enter long. The trade went brilliantly, confirming my belief in high-confluence scenarios.

TRADE EXECUTION STRATEGIES

Executing a trade requires more than just pressing the buy or sell button. It's a deliberate process that necessitates meticulous planning and exact timing. Below are some best practices:

- **Use Pending Orders:** Instead of manually making trades, try using pending orders, such as purchase limits or sell stops. These orders ensure that your trade is only performed at the desired price level.

- **Wait for Retests:** After a breakout, let the price to retest the breakout level before entering. The risk of a false breakout is reduced as a result.

- **Avoid Chasing the Market:** If you miss an entry, do not chase the price. Wait for another setup to align with your strategy.

I made a mistake early on by pursuing a breakout on the USD/CAD pair. The price had already risen significantly from the breakout level, but I entered nonetheless, worried I might miss out. Predictably, the market reversed, and I was stopped out. That loss taught me to wait for proper retests and avoid making rash trading decisions.

BALANCING PRECISION AND FLEXIBILITY

While exact timing is critical, remaining flexible is also important. Markets are dynamic, and rigidly adhering to a single strategy might result in missed chances or excessive losses. Be prepared to adjust to changing conditions, but always within the parameters of your trading strategy.

A perfect illustration of blending precision and flexibility came during a tumultuous session on the USD/JPY pair. My

PRICE ACTION DAY TRADING

original strategy was to enter after a bullish breakout and retest. However, as the breakout took place, I noted exceptionally high volume and a powerful momentum candle. I altered my strategy and joined earlier than expected, capitalizing on the momentum. The trade was successful, but it served as a reminder to be adaptable.

Timing and entry precision distinguish great traders from average ones. Mastering confirmation signals, various timeframe analysis, high-confluence setups, and strategic execution can help you greatly increase your trading performance. Remember that accurate timing demands patience and discipline, both of which are developed with practice and experience.

SIX

TECHNICAL INDICATORS AND PRICE ACTION

While price action is the foundation of successful trading, technical indicators can be useful tools in your decision-making process. When used appropriately, indicators can provide extra insights and assist corroborate price action signals, making your trades more reliable.

This chapter delves into the importance of moving averages, momentum oscillators, and volume analysis approaches in aligning with price action strategies. I'll also give a personal anecdote on how combining indicators and price action turned a difficult trading situation rewarding.

COMPLEMENTARY INDICATOR SELECTION

Indicators should supplement, not replace, price action analysis. Choosing indicators that align with your strategy and trading style is crucial. Using too many indicators might clog your charts and cause analysis paralysis, but using too few may result in analysis gaps. The best method is to use indicators that provide unique and meaningful information.

Some often used complimentary indicators are:

- **Moving Averages:** Used to identify trends and dynamic support/resistance levels.
- **The Relative Strength Index (RSI):** Overbought and oversold situations are measured by the Relative Strength Index (RSI).
- **MACD (Moving Average Convergence Divergence):** A trend-following and momentum indicator.

- **Volume Indicators:** Used to analyze market involvement and potential reversals.

One error I made early in my trading career was overloading my chart with indicators. I had Bollinger Bands, RSI, MACD, and Stochastic Oscillators all on the same chart, expecting that additional indicators would result in better trades. Instead, I became confused and missed apparent price action indications. Simplifying my setup and focusing on the indicators that genuinely brought value made all the difference.

MOVING AVERAGES IN PRICE ACTION CONTEXT.

Moving averages are useful instruments that integrate well with price action. They assist in identifying trends, providing dynamic support and resistance levels, and filtering out market noise. Common types include:

- **Simple Moving Average (SMA):** A straightforward average of previous prices.
- **Exponential Moving Average (EMA):** Increases the weight of recent prices, making it more responsive to changes.

For example, a 50-period EMA can be used as a trend filter. If the price is regularly above the EMA, it indicates an uptrend, but prices below it indicates a decline.

Moving averages can also serve as the foundation for crossover strategies, in which a shorter-term moving average crossing above a longer-term one indicates a probable bullish trend.

In a recent trade, I used the 20-period EMA to confirm a decline in the GBP/USD pair. The price retraced to the EMA, forming a bullish pin bar before continuing its upward trend. Combining the EMA with price action allowed me to enter at the appropriate time and ride the trend securely.

MOMENTUM OSCILLATORS

Momentum oscillators, such as the RSI and Stochastic Oscillator, quantify the strength and speed of price changes. These indicators are very helpful in recognizing overbought and oversold circumstances, as well as probable reversals.

- **Relative Strength Index:** The RSI spans from 0 to 100, with readings above 70 suggesting overbought conditions and values below 30 indicating oversold levels. Divergences between the RSI and price action may indicate upcoming reversals.

- The Stochastic Oscillator is similar to the RSI but more sensitive; it compares the closing price to the price range over a given time period. It works best in a wide range of markets.

I recall a trade on the EUR/JPY pair in which the RSI indicated divergence. While the price was making greater highs, the RSI was making lower highs, indicating a slowing bullish momentum. I had the confidence to enter a short trade because this divergence corresponded with a resistance zone and a bearish engulfing candle. The market reversed as expected, confirming my belief in momentum oscillators.

VOLUME ANALYSIS TECHNIQUES

Volume is the market's heartbeat. It shows the level of engagement and can reveal important information about the strength of a trend or the likelihood of a reversal. The key volume concepts include

- Rising volume indicates the strength of a trend or breakout.

- **Diverging Volume:** When the price rises while the volume falls, it indicates a probable reversal.

- Volume spikes frequently occur during key turning events, such as breakouts or reversals.

One of my most memorable trades featured volume analysis of the USD/CAD pair. The price had been stabilizing near a resistance level on dwindling volume. Suddenly, a volume spike happened during a breakout, indicating high participation. I entered the trade and profited handsomely as the momentum continued. This experience taught me to recognise the importance of volume in confirming price action signals.

INTEGRATING INDICATORS AND PRICE ACTION

The true magic happens when indicators and price action collaborate. For example:

- Use RSI or Stochastic to validate reversal patterns such as double bottoms or head and shoulders.

- To identify pullback entry, combine moving averages and candlestick patterns.
- Use volume to validate breakouts or trend continuations.

Always keep in mind that indicators should be used as support. Your primary emphasis should be on price action, as it provides the clearest and most immediate indication of market sentiment.

I recall a trade on the AUD/USD pair that constituted a watershed moment in my trading career. I had detected a probable breakout through price action, but I was hesitant to enter owing to previous losses from fake breakouts. This time, I choose to employ volume as a confirmation method. When the breakout coincided with a substantial volume spike, I entered the trade with confidence. The market moved quickly in my favor, and I reached my target within hours. That trade not only increased my account balance, but also improved my understanding of how indicators may complement price action.

When applied appropriately, technical indicators can be extremely useful. You can improve your trading judgements and confidence by choosing complimentary indicators, understanding their context, and combining them with price action. Maintain a clean chart, focus on simplicity, and always use price action as your guiding principle.

The following chapter will go over the vital process of building a trading plan, which is a necessary step towards gaining consistency and long-term success in trading.

SEVEN

TRADING PLAN DEVELOPMENT

A well-structured trading plan is the foundation for consistent success in day trading. Trading without a plan becomes an emotional rollercoaster, leading to rash judgements and excessive loss. Chapter 8 focusses on designing a personalized trading blueprint, tracking performance, backtesting strategies, and developing long-term profitable habits. I'll also tell you a personal experience of how a disciplined trading plan can alter your life.

CREATING A PERSONAL TRADING BLUEPRINT

A trading blueprint serves as a road map, detailing your goals, strategies, and guidelines. Here's how to make one.

- **Define Your Goals:** Set precise, quantifiable, and realistic trading goals. Are you looking for a set monthly percentage gain, or are you focusing on mastering strategies?

- **Select Trading Strategies:** Decide which strategies you'll employ, such as pin bars, breakouts, or trend-following setups.

- **Establish Risk Management Rules:** Determine your risk per trade, maximum daily loss limit, and reward-to-risk ratio.

- **Set Trade Criteria:** Outline the conditions for entering and leaving trades, including confirmation signals and preferred timeframes.

- **Choose Your Tools:** Choose the technical indicators, charting software, and other tools that best align with your strategy.

When I first started trading, I hopped from strategy to strategy, hoping to find a quick formula for success. It wasn't until I devised a precise trading plan that I started seeing consistent results. The plan provided me with clarity and structure, reducing guesswork and emotional decisions.

PERFORMANCE TRACKING AND JOURNALING

Tracking your performance is critical for understanding your strengths, limitations, and opportunities for improvement. A trading log is your closest friend throughout this process. Here is what to include:

- Trade details include the date, time, asset, entry and exit locations, position size, and outcome.
- Consider the rationale for each trade, including price action signals and confluence variables.
- **Emotional State:** Record your emotions before, during, and after the trade to detect psychological patterns.
- Calculate the profit or loss and determine whether the trade followed your plan.

One of my breakthrough moments occurred when checking my trading log. I observed a pattern: my losses frequently occurred when I veered from my plan or allowed my emotions to guide my actions. Addressing these patterns helped me increase my discipline and consistency.

BACKTESTING AND STRATEGY REFINEMENT

To evaluate the efficacy of your strategies, backtesting includes testing them against past data. This procedure allows you to acquire confidence in your strategy and then refine it based on the results. Take these steps:

- **Select A Strategy:** Select a particular strategy to test, such as an inside bar setup.
- **Collect Data:** Utilize historical charts from your favorite markets and timeframes.
- **Simulate Trades:** Run the strategy on the data, documenting the entry, exit, and outcome for each trade.

- **Analyze The Results:** Determine the strategy's win rate, average reward-to-risk ratio, and overall profitability

I spent weeks backtesting a breakout strategy for the EUR/USD pair. While the win percentage was reasonable, I noted that trades using other confluence elements, like as volume spikes or major support/resistance levels, performed substantially better. Incorporating these findings into my plan improved the strategy's success rate.

DEVELOPING CONSISTENT TRADING HABITS

Consistency is the key to long-term trading success. *Here are some crucial behaviors to cultivate:*

- **Stick To Your Plan:** Even if attracted by impetuous opportunities, avoid departing from your trading blueprint.
- **Set a Routine:** Create a daily trading schedule that includes pre-market analysis, trade execution, and post-market review.

PRICE ACTION DAY TRADING

- Mindfulness and emotional management can help you stay focused and disciplined.
- **Continuous Learning:** Commit to continuing your knowledge through books, classes, and market research.

I will never forget the day I chose to approach trading like a company. I made a planned timetable, set daily targets, and followed my plan religiously. These habits gradually improved my approach and outcomes, transforming trading from a tedious pastime into a consistent source of revenue.

Early in my trading career, I suffered a substantial loss owing to a lack of discipline and strategy. Frustrated and determined to improve, I resolved to develop a thorough trading plan and stick to it no matter what. The first week was difficult—I missed impetuous trades that may have paid well, but I also averted several possible losses.

One specific trade stands out. I noticed a textbook inside bar setup on the GBP/USD daily chart. My plan required a breakout confirmation, but I was eager to enter first. I waited while remembering my devotion to the plan. The breakout ultimately arrived, and I entered with confidence, resulting in

47

a significant profit. That trade emphasized the importance of discipline and confirmed my trading plan.

A trading plan is more than just a series of rules; it provides the cornerstone for long-term success. You may navigate the markets with confidence and discipline by generating a personalized blueprint, tracking your performance, backtesting strategies, and developing consistent routines.

In the following chapter, we'll examine the broader market backdrop and economic factors that drive price action, allowing you to adjust to changing conditions and exploit new possibilities.

EIGHT

MARKET CONTEXT AND ECONOMIC CONSIDERATIONS

Understanding the larger market environment is critical for any trader seeking to excel at price action trading. Forex markets are constantly changing and significantly influenced by global economic conditions, geopolitical events, and session-specific factors.

This chapter digs into the important features of market context, including the impact of economic news on price action, session-based trading strategies, and reacting to changing market conditions. I'll also discuss a personal experience that taught me the value of remaining updated about market trends.

UNDERSTANDING FOREX MARKET DYNAMICS.

Forex trading takes place in a worldwide, decentralized market where currencies are traded around the clock. Supply and demand drive the market, with central bank policies, economic data releases, and geopolitical happenings all having an impact. To trade effectively, you must first grasp these characteristics and their impact on price movement

- **Central Bank Policies:** Interest rate choices, quantitative easing, and other monetary policies have a direct impact on currency values. For example, when a central bank announces a rate hike, its currency often strengthens.
- **Economic Indicators:** GDP growth, employment data, inflation rates, and trade balances provide information about a country's economic health, which influences currency strength.

- Geopolitical events such as elections, trade wars, and natural disasters can produce major market volatility and influence price action.

Early in my trading career, I overestimated the importance of market dynamics. I traded the EUR/USD pair during a quiet period, only for the price to unexpectedly jump following a European Central Bank announcement. That experience taught me to always monitor the economic calendar and stay up to current on important events.

THE EFFECT OF ECONOMIC NEWS ON PRICE ACTION

Economic news releases are among the most important factors influencing short-term price changes. Events such as non-farm payrolls, central bank meetings, and inflation figures can cause significant volatility. As a price action trader, you must be aware of these events and understand how they affect the market.

- Focus on news releases that are designated as having a major impact on economic calendars. These events frequently produce huge price fluctuations and trading opportunities.

- Avoid entering trades just before important news releases unless you have a clear advantage.
- **Post-News Reaction:** Allow the market to digest the news before watching price action for potential setups.

I recall making a trade on the USD/JPY pair during the announcement of US jobs data. The market first surged higher, triggering stop-loss orders, before reversing and forming a strong negative trend. Waiting for the news reaction to calm allowed me to identify a high-probability entry and capitalize on it.

SESSION-BASED TRADING STRATEGIES.

The forex market has three primary trading sessions: Asian, European, and North American. Each session has specific characteristics that influence price action:

- **Asian Session:** Typically quieter, with smaller price ranges and lower volatility. Ideal for range-based strategies.
- The European session is known for its strong liquidity and large price changes as major financial centers open.

- The North American session overlaps with the European session, resulting in the most active and volatile hour of the trading day.

Session-based strategies enable you to customize your approach to the unique conditions of each trading period. For example, during the European session, breakout strategies may be more profitable due to heightened volatility, but the Asian session favors mean-reversion setups.

One of my most profitable trades happened during the London-New York session overlap. I noticed a breakout pattern on the GBP/USD pair as the market reacted to surprise UK inflation data. The additional liquidity during this overlap accelerated the movement, resulting in a swift and lucrative trade.

ADAPTING TO CHANGING MARKET CONDITIONS.

Markets are continuously changing, making adaptability a vital trait for traders. Changes in volatility, attitude, or broader economic trends can all cause conditions to shift. Here's how to maintain agility:

- **Monitor Volatility:** Use tools such as Average True Range (ATR) to assess market volatility and alter your strategies accordingly.

- **Stay Informed:** To predict market moves, follow economic news, central bank pronouncements, and geopolitical happenings.

- **Adjust Risk Management:** During times of high volatility, consider lowering position sizes or broadening stop-loss levels to account for larger price swings.

During the COVID-19 pandemic, I realized how important adaptability was. Forex markets were extremely volatile, and strategies that worked under steady conditions failed. I was able to navigate the turbulence and secure my account by modifying my approach, focusing on shorter timeframes and prioritizing risk management.

One noteworthy event highlights the necessity of understanding market context. I was trading EUR/GBP and saw a strong bullish trend. I entered a long position without first reviewing the news, only to watch the price drop moments later. The Bank of England had unexpectedly slashed interest rates, which weakened the pound.

That loss served as a wake-up call. From that point forward, I resolved to keep updated about market-moving events. This habit not only enhanced my trading results, but it also increased my understanding of how economic issues influence price action.

Trading is more than just technical analysis; it's about understanding the big picture. Staying updated about market dynamics, analyzing the impact of economic news, customizing your strategies to different trading sessions, and responding to changing conditions will allow you to make better judgements and increase your trading success.

CONCLUSION

THE PATH TO TRADING MASTERY

The path to mastering price action trading involves continuous learning, practice, and adaptation. As we wrap up this book, it's critical to synthesize the strategies, principles, and methodologies we've covered. This final chapter provides a guide to solidifying your knowledge, adopting a lifelong learning mindset, and developing consistency for long-term success. Along the process, I'll tell a personal narrative that exemplifies the essence of trading mastery.

SYNTHESIZING LEARNT STRATEGIES

Throughout this book, we've discussed a variety of price action trading strategies and fundamental ideas. Every strategy you've learnt, from reading candlestick patterns to spotting high-confluence trade scenarios, contributes to the overall picture. To properly integrate these strategies into your trading, take the following steps:

- **Review and Reassess:** Review your trading plan on a regular basis to ensure that it fits with the knowledge you've acquired.
- **Focus on Your Strengths:** Identify and perfect the strategies that work best for your trading style.
- Use complementing tools like as technical indicators or session-based strategies to get an advantage.

In my own trading career, the process of synthesizing strategies marked a turning point. I originally tried numerous ways, which resulted in confusion and inconsistencies. It wasn't until I focused on mastering a few fundamental settings, such as the pin bar and breakout strategies, that I started seeing consistent results.

CONTINUOUS LEARNING AND ADAPTATION.

The forex market is continually changing, influenced by technical improvements, economic shifts, and changing trader behavior. To stay ahead, adopt the mindset of a continual learner. *Here are some techniques to sustain your growth:*

- **Stay Curious:** Continue to investigate new strategies, market trends, and tools.
- **Learn from Others:** Join trading communities, study books, and follow successful traders.
- **Adapt to Market Conditions:** Be adaptable in your approach, modifying your strategies to fit the current market climate.

There was a period when my trading performance plateaued. Frustrated but motivated, I took an advanced price action trading course. The knowledge I learnt revived my passion and provided me with new perspectives, allowing me to adapt and improve my trading.

ESTABLISHING LONG-TERM TRADING CONSISTENCY

A successful trader is known for his or her consistency. It is not about achieving perfection, but about staying disciplined, controlling risk, and carrying out your plan over time. *Here are some important concepts for developing consistency:*

- **Stick To Your Plan:** Even during instances of uncertainty, avoid deviating from your trading blueprint.
- **Embrace Risk Management:** Protect your capital by staying within your specified risk limitations.
- **Focus on Process, Not Outcome:** Rather than worrying about profits or losses, concentrate on correctly completing trades.

One of my most transforming moments happened during a long losing streak. Instead of abandoning my plan, I examined my notebook and discovered minor flaws in execution. By resolving these difficulties and keeping disciplined, I gradually reversed the tide, finishing the month on a profitable streak.

During my early days as a trader, I frequently found myself pursuing the promise of quick riches. I entered trades rashly, overleveraged my positions, and overlooked the necessity of risk management. Inevitably, these habits resulted in a considerable drop in my confidence.

Determined to recuperate, I returned to the fundamentals. I spent weeks backtesting strategies, perfecting my trading plan, and committing to logging every trade. One day, I noticed a fantastic inside bar setup on the EUR/USD daily chart. Following my detailed plan, I entered the trade with measured risk and defined exit points. The trade went perfectly, supporting my confidence in the value of discipline and strategy.

That incident signaled the start of a shift in my approach. I realized that trading mastery isn't about forecasting every market move; it's about sticking to a well-thought-out plan with consistency and confidence.

THE FUTURE OF PRICE ACTION TRADING

The future of price action trading seems promising, with opportunities evolving alongside market trends and technologies. While the basics of price action are ageless, innovations like AI-driven analytics and algorithmic trading provide traders with new tools. Accept these developments while remaining grounded in the fundamental principles of price action trading.

As you continue, keep in mind that your adventure is far from over. Trading is a lifelong pursuit full with obstacles and rewards. Maintain your patience, persistence, and willingness to grow.

FINAL WORDS

Price action trading is more than just a concept; it is a discipline that allows you to traverse the forex markets with ease and confidence. You are prepared to go on a path to consistent profitability and trading mastery by mastering the strategies, principles, and mindset taught in this book.

Remember that success in trading is determined by the sustainability of your achievements rather than the pace with which you improve. Maintain discipline, curiosity, and trust in the process. The markets will always provide opportunities; your preparation and mindset will decide your success.

Thank you for letting me be your guide on this adventure. As you implement these teachings and embark on your path to trading mastery, I wish you success and fulfilment.

GET INSTANT ACCESS TO THE FREE VIDEO COURSE BY CLICKING OR COPYING AND PASTING THE LINK BELOW TO YOUR BROWSER!!

https://mailchi.mp/8465a286d83d/chinedu-brown-fx

Happy Watching!!

www.ingramcontent.com/pod-product-compliance
Lightning Source LLC
Chambersburg PA
CBHW071108240526
45469CB00006BD/2392